IMAGES OF ENGLAND

ICKENHAM

IMAGES OF ENGLAND

ICKENHAM

JAMES SKINNER

TEMPUS

This book is dedicated to the memory of my brother Kevin – a resident of Ickenham for many years.

Frontispiece: A newspaper advertisement dated June 1935, announcing the extensive property development of land adjoining Ivy House Farm, where new homes could be purchased for a mere 52p a week! This was only one of many new estates that had been built since 1923, and more were to follow.

First published 2005

Tempus Publishing Limited
The Mill, Brimscombe Port,
Stroud, Gloucestershire, GL5 2QG
www.tempus-publishing.com

© James Skinner, 2005

The right of James Skinner to be identified as the Author
of this work has been asserted in accordance with the
Copyrights, Designs and Patents Act 1988.

British Library Cataloguing in Publication Data.
A catalogue record for this book is available from the British Library.

ISBN 0 7524 3411 X

Typesetting and origination by Tempus Publishing Limited.
Printed in Great Britain.

Contents

Acknowledgements

As always, I am indebted to the *Uxbridge Gazette* for generously granting permission to use their archive photographs.

Also to Carolynne Cotton and Gwyn Jones of the Heritage Department, Uxbridge Central Library for their help with my research and for the loan of their photographs.

My sincere thanks are due also to the following people who provided me with information for the compilation of this book, especially those who kindly supplied pictures from their private collections and allowed them to be reproduced here: Barbara Buckle, John Huse, Susan and David Crane, Trevor Jaggar, Janet, Alan and Tim Noad, Malcolm Parsons, Pat Sparke, Bob Hamer, Geoff Shew, Keith Chamberlain, Tony Thrasher, Marjorie Brooks, Rayner Heyd, Philip Rutter, Freda and Ralph Smith, David Millen, Susan Atkins, Tony Caulkett, George Richman, John and Oliver Inwards, Diana May, Jim Foley, Freddy Staff, Perry Parsons, Pamela Barnard, Linda West, Charles Williams, Janet Taylor, Margaret Puckey, Barry Twigg, Eric Goodall, Ken Pearce, Sylvia Taylor, Tim Leman, Alan Edwards, Peter Daymond, Chris Berry, Toby Vandevelde, Barbara Fisher.

Finally, my grateful thanks to Elaine Verweymeren for processing the manuscript.

Introduction

'A very pleasant place' was how renowned diarist Samuel Pepys described Swakeleys Manor after visiting the estate in 1665. His assessment could have applied to the village itself, for the Ickenham landscape of long ago was a pleasant composition of thick woodlands, secluded farmsteads, rich pastures and meadows adorned with wild flowers. Leafy lanes screened by avenues of stately elms, the straggling Pinn Brook skirting the fields, and overhead birdsong completed this idyllic setting. Fortunately a few relics of that bygone age still remain – principally Swakeleys House and the even more ancient parish church of St Giles.

The earliest recognition of Ickenham appeared in the Domesday Book of 1086, which referred to it as Ticheham, and many more variations of the name were mentioned in Public Record Office documents of the 1300s. The Domesday Book also recorded three estates in the area, and it is thought that two of them became the Manor of Ickenham, while the third (and largest) formed the nucleus of Swakeleys, which derived its name from the first owner Robert de Swalclyve (*c.* 1326).

In the centuries that followed, while the Lords of both Manors came and went, the main occupations were dairy farming and agriculture. By 1801, the population numbered a mere 213, but the peace and serenity of the sleepy hamlet could not last forever, and the turn of the twentieth century heralded significant changes that meant the village was destined to lose its rural image of old world charm. After the arrival of the Metropolitan Railway in 1905, Ickenham's green and pleasant land gradually succumbed to large scale property development. In 1922, the 300-acre Swakeleys estate was sold by auction. In addition to the Jacobean mansion, it comprised nine farms, nineteen cottages, building land and smallholdings. Acres of woodland were cleared; meadows mown down; and one by one the farms eventually disappeared. In their place, several housing estates sprang up, not only in the Swakeleys region but also in a large area around Ickenham Green and on the other side of the railway tracks near the Glebe. New roads were laid, which at first remained unmade-up dirt tracks resembling dust bowls in summer and quagmires in winter. In time they became attractive tree-lined avenues with neat rows of bungalows and houses – the age of suburbia had arrived.

Building programmes continued throughout the 1930s, as hundreds of people moved into the area, attracted by the railway company's and developers' advertisements for cheaper homes in the countryside. In 1933, houses were offered at under £500, and a monthly season ticket to London (journey time 40 minutes) cost £1 14s. The Second World War in 1939 brought a temporary halt to this march of progress, but it resumed in the 1950s and 1960s. In the period from 1930 to 1962, five new schools and a church were erected in addition to shopping parades and hundreds of private dwellings. The population increased steadily from 329 in 1901 to well over 11,000 by 1986.

The once familiar pastoral scene of cows wending their way along Ickenham's country lanes has now given way to one of endless streams of traffic on the two main roads through the centre of the village. Newcomers could not possibly envisage the tranquillity that once prevailed. But although it is now regarded as more suburb than village, Ickenham has retained a strong sense of camaraderie and community spirit associated with village life. Neighbours not only get on well together – they actually like each other. Deprived of a once promised cinema and lacking other entertainment facilities enjoyed by their near neighbours at Ruislip and Uxbridge, the villagers became rather good at providing their own amusement, and consequently a wide variety of organisations came into being – most of which are still thriving. Maybe everything in the Ickenham garden isn't always lovely, but whenever problems arise, the residents are always prepared to band together and fight their corner against adversity. And over the years several campaigns have been waged and won to preserve Ickenham history and heritage.

Although Ickenham may have been regarded as an unimportant backwater where nothing much happens, it can at least claim to have enjoyed more than the proverbial 'fifteen minutes of fame'. The village has been privileged to entertain royalty on a number of occasions, beginning with Queen Mary's visits to Swakeleys Manor in the late 1920s, followed by those of HRH Prince Philip in 1977 and 1985. HRH Prince Edward came to reopen the Compass Theatre in 1990, and returned in 2002 with Countess Sophie to attend Glebe School's golden jubilee. HRH Princess Anne was a guest of Douay Martyrs School, as were the late Cardinal Hume and Chris Patten. In addition to Samuel Pepys, another house guest at Swakeleys was the librettist W.S. Gilbert who is reputed to have worked on the libretto of *Iolanthe* while staying there in 1882.

Film actor Sabu (of *Elephant Boy* fame) lived in Swakeleys Lodge while filming at Denham Studios, and Jean Simmons, his co-star in *Black Narcissus* visited the community centre in 1950. Other personalities from the entertainment world came to Ickenham on social occasions, among them Bobby Howes, Florence de Jong, Ena Baga, Judith Chalmers and Roy Castle. While television presenter Sue Cook returns frequently to the scene of her childhood, which is still – to quote Mr Pepys – 'a very pleasant place'.

A sentiment with which most would agree.

James Skinner

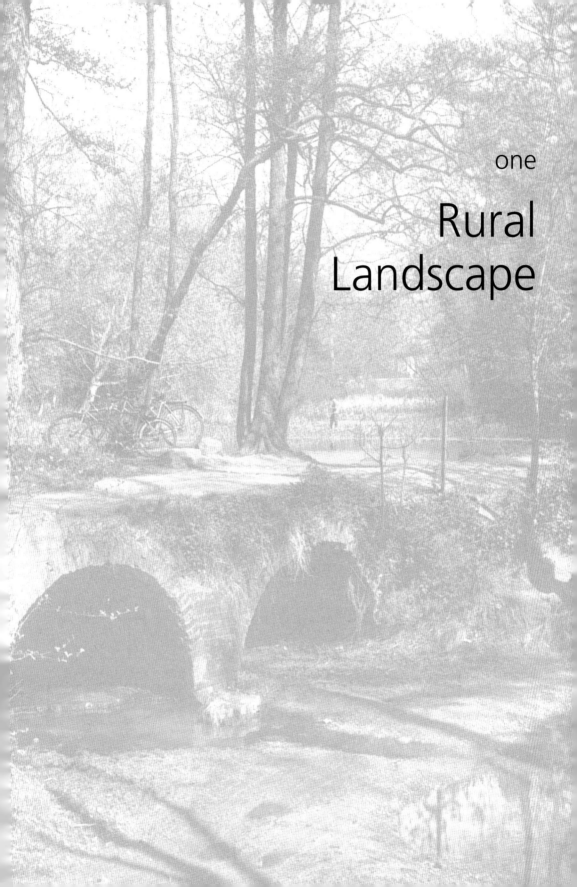

one

Rural Landscape

Above: This early twentieth-century view of Ickenham village is a perfect example of the serene tranquillity prevailing at the time. On the left is the original Fox and Geese public house, and standing behind the pond is Home Farm house, which dates from the Tudor period.

Left: Another picturesque scene typifying the village's rural image shows the footpath leading from Back Lane (now Swakeleys Road) through the field used by Ickenham Cricket Club until 1928. It led eventually to Milton Farm which was demolished in 1939 to make way for Milton Court and Milton Road. The path was roughly where Ivy House Road is today.

A familiar landmark in the heart of Swakeleys woods during the 1920s and 1930s was this two–arched bridge straddling what was known as The Splash, created by the overflow from the River Pinn. Its approximate location was at the meeting point of Warren Road and Swakeleys Drive.

The bridge in 1934 without the rustic latticework, as most people remember it. The Splash was a favourite spot with youngsters fishing for tiddlers, and the surrounding area ideal for walkers and blackberry pickers. It survived until 1957.

Probably the most prominent landmark in the village is the Ickenham Pump, which takes centre stage in this 1928 photograph. It was bequeathed to the inhabitants by local benefactress Charlotte Gell. In 1866, a 144ft-deep well was sunk enabling many villagers to enjoy a supply of fresh water for the first time. The pond was enlarged to accommodate waste from the pump, which remained in use until the end of 1914, and was eventually sealed in 1921. The former post office can be seen on the left of the picture, with the Church Farm buildings on the right.

A 1930 view from the pond of the old Fox and Geese Inn which dated from the nineteenth century. Its name board is advertising 'Harman's Ales and Stout' – brewed in neighbouring Uxbridge. The front of the Church of England school, erected in 1866, can be seen to the left of the public house. Both buildings were demolished in 1934 when Ickenham High Road was widened.

It is 1931, and the pond is sporting a brand new set of railings, even if only on one side. The fourteenth-century parish church of St Giles – the oldest building in Ickenham – stands opposite with the pump to its left. It is interesting to note the contrasting styles of weathervane on the two buildings with the letter 'G' in memory of Charlotte Gell topping the pump's ornate canopy, and the golden cockerel (formerly mounted on the coach house at Swakeleys Manor) perched on the church's timber bell turret.

The pond during the 1970s, looking more cluttered with vegetation than in its early years. Another set of railings has been erected, and a red telephone box has replaced the original white kiosk that was the first to be installed in the village in the 1920s.

A section of Swakeleys Road photographed in August 1930. The junction with Breakspear Road South is just out of the left of the picture. Originally known as Weston Lane in the eighteenth century, the road was renamed Back Lane during the Victorian era and acquired its present name in 1928.

The same scene a few years later. A complete row of houses has sprung up along Swakeleys Road as far as Derwent Avenue. More development followed and, by 1937, houses had been erected on the other side of the road, which was converted to a dual carriageway.

Another part of Swakeleys Road around 1930, at the point where Woodstock Drive joined it almost thirty years later. The sign on the left by the telegraph pole is advertising the Harefield Place Country Club, with its facilities for tennis and golf. Situated at the end of The Drive, the club was originally a seventeenth-century mansion and, in 1936, was converted to Uxbridge Country (convalescent) Hospital.

A passer-by stops to chat to workmen engaged in felling the giant elms at the junction of Swakeleys Road and The Avenue in 1936. The trees were sacrificed during the process of eradicating the sharp bend prior to constructing the dual carriageway. Ivy House Farm can be seen on the extreme left.

Ickenham High Road, around 1932, looking towards West Ruislip. The two cyclists have complete freedom of the road, which was widened shortly afterwards. Judging by this picture, it hardly seemed necessary!

The Avenue looking in a very sorry state in December 1935. A tradesman's horse and cart are struggling through a morass of mud and water, while the two boy cyclists appear to be bogged down. Evidently many of Ickenham's roads were in a similar condition at the time.

Right: An avenue of stately Douglas firs (some of which still survive) was a feature of Warren Road in this 1930s picture. The road, which was carved out of the woods of Swakeleys Park in the mid-1920s after the estate had been sold, remained un-made up for many years. It derived its name from the 46-acre Warren Farm – part of the nearby Harefield Place estate. The farm was so named because of its proximity to an immense rabbit warren, which, in 1810, was said to be the largest in the county.

Below: Swakeleys Road is awash during the last week of January 1936, as a London Transport bus on the No. 220 route from Uxbridge to Pinner, ploughs its way through the floods created by the river Pinn. The Pinn, which has a notorious track record of flooding, had burst its banks in several places, and many houses and gardens nearby were flooded. The arches of the road bridge were completely submerged as the torrent of water surged underneath. In April 1936, the No. 220 service was re-routed via Hercies Road and Long Lane on its way to Ickenham, and in its place route No. 223 was introduced to accommodate Swakeleys Road passengers. It survived until 1989, when being replaced by the U1 service.

The village centre in February 1936, showing the new police box in the foreground. After its installation, the *Middlesex Advertiser* commented that 'the accumulation of objects around the village pump is being added to from time to time, without adding much to the old charm of the village scene, and the latest is the police box in the foreground which hides the Girl Guides' Jubilee tree just behind'. Presumably, the report was referring to the 'Keep Left' obelisks, a lamp-post, signpost and Belisha beacons marking the crossing, in addition to the telephone and police boxes. However, the 'objects' could have been considered useful assets to the general public.

Three months later, on 4 May 1936, the police telephone box system came into operation in the Uxbridge Sub-division of the Metropolitan Police. The picture shows the scene of the first trial, in which a wireless car and utility van capable of dealing with accidents were summoned from the box and were on the spot in just over five minutes. The public was invited to make full use of these boxes in case of an emergency, but unfortunately they are no longer in use. Perhaps they would have been an asset in the current climate of rising crime.

An isolated lay-by in Austins Lane during the summer of 1948, where two motorists are evidently conserving their petrol allocation. Rationing continued for a further two years, and when it ended, the price per gallon rose to 3s – the highest since 1920.

Glebe Avenue in 1949, when it still had the appearance of a country lane and children could play safely on the road. Note the two boys with their home-made kiddie car. The avenue, originally known as Marsh Lane, then Glebe Lane, derived its name from the 'glebe' or church land, part of the common fields stretching to Ickenham Marsh. In the seventeenth century a rectory, then known as The Parsonage, was built here, being leased as a farm in 1750. Thus Glebe Farm came into being and farm workers' cottages still survive in the road. Many more changes followed, and Glebe Avenue can now boast an Underground Railway station; several new housing estates; an elementary school; two shopping parades and a 'little theatre'. However, one new project that failed to materialize was a cinema.

Above: On a raw day during the severe winter of 1955, an undeterred John Hardinge from The Avenue appears to be revelling in the harsh conditions, as, fully equipped with all the gear, he imagines skiing down an Alpine slope. In reality he is in Swakeleys woods.

Left: By contrast, a housewife with her shopping basket trudging through the snow by the lakeside on her way to the shops is probably less enchanted by the inclement weather.

The snows of 1955 provided the photographer with another opportunity to produce an attractive Christmas card effect in a Swakeleys woodland setting, and prove that Ickenham still retained its rural image.

'Totem Pole Avenue' is how residents of The Grove described the road in October 1976, after the branches had been lopped off their elm trees – dying from Dutch elm disease. The grotesque figures awaiting final execution prompted the local press to comment that 'the stump-lined road is fast losing its charm'. Then two Norwegian maples were planted at the residents' expense, but other replacement trees failed to thrive. However, the residents again came to the rescue and replanted a variety of species including alders, chestnuts, beech, ginkgo and tulip trees, which have helped to restore the avenue to its former beauty.

The lower end of Warren road in 1958. Tree fellers and bulldozers have created a large clearing in the woods in preparation for the extensions to Swakeleys Drive and Warren Road. All traces of The Splash and its bridge have disappeared, and Woodstock Drive is in the course of construction.

This view from almost the same spot looking towards Swakeleys Drive was taken nearly twenty years later – in February 1976. The parapet of the replacement bridge is on the extreme right, while a tantalising glimpse of Swakeleys House can be seen through the trees beside the lake.

A group of young voluntary workers helping to clean the River Pinn in 1976. After a long dry spell, the water level is well down, enabling the volunteers to get to grips with the job in hand.

On a bleak, overcast day, the meandering Pinn is now flowing freely, unhampered by weeds and debris.

Two local lads are thoroughly enjoying themselves, 'messing about on the river'. Only it isn't a river, of course, merely Derwent Avenue on a bad day – 17 August 1977, to be precise. Once again, the swollen Pinn was the culprit, its floodwaters rising to more than 3ft. At least a dozen houses in the road were flooded to a depth of 5in.

A 1978 composite picture of three of Ickenham's most familiar landmarks. On the left is the house formerly known as Little Buntings – now converted into offices; St Giles's church is in the centre and the pump is on the extreme right.

two

Down
on the Farm

Home Farm, a fifteenth-century timber-framed building with additions made in 1705. Known as Church Place in 1624 when owned by the Crosier family, it passed to the Hilliards and eventually the Saich family in the late nineteenth century, acquiring the name Home Farm in 1887. After Cyril Saich's death in 1989, the farm was sold and the Church Place apartments were built on land adjacent to the house in 1993.

A view from the farmyard looking towards Ickenham High Road. Home Farm House is in the centre of the picture, and part of St Giles's church can be seen on the left.

Above: Cyril Saich with one of his Poll steers at Slough Cattle Show in the 1930s, having to be content with second prize on this occasion. He exhibited regularly at various agricultural shows including nearby Uxbridge, and won prizes at Smithfield. Cyril, who took over Home Farm in 1927, was one of a family of eight boys and a girl. His grandfather Matthew was at one time licensee of the Coach and Horses, and two brothers Algernon and Len both kept shops in the village. Cyril was married to May Wiskin, daughter of a former owner of the village shop.

Right: The front cover of Cyril Saich's customer order book. He supplied three types of milk, two of butter, cream and eggs. Until 1946, he operated four delivery rounds after which he concentrated on his pedigree herd of Aberdeen Angus beef cattle.

Left: A wartime photograph of Pat Sparke (*née* Byrne) in her Women's Land Army uniform. London-born Pat joined the WLA in 1941, and after training at Sparsholt Agricultural College, was assigned to Home Farm where she worked for Cyril Saich until 1946. After a brief return to her pre-war office job in Willesden, she decided that she belonged 'down on the farm' and returned to Ickenham, where she virtually managed the business for Mr Saich. In addition, she cared for Mrs Saich until her death in 1964, and then for her ailing employer who died in 1989. A former Company Girl Guide leader, Pat is the longest serving member of Ickenham WI, which she joined in 1947.

Below: The dairy on the right of this picture is where Pat spent many of her working hours. The farmhouse is on the left, and cattle sheds are beyond the gate in the centre.

A rear view of Manor Farm in 1908. This was the principal manor of Ickenham, and was known as Ickenham Hall until around 1820. The present building dates from the sixteenth century, with several modifications being made in succeeding centuries.

A 1980 photograph of the Manor House, complete with tennis courts. Various lords of the manor throughout the ages included the Shorediche family, Thomas Truesdale Clarke and the last holder, David Pool, who died in 1956. Manorial rights were then vested in the Borough of Uxbridge.

Ivy House Farm, Swakeleys Road in the 1930s. Early records prior to 1780 list the owner as Revd Thomas Clarke, but information on subsequent owners is not readily available. However, in the early part of the twentieth century, the farm was purchased by the then tenant Alfred Pool, and it became known as Pool's Dairy.

Ivy House Farm's magnificent Ancient Barn, which was a much-admired landmark on the bend of Swakeleys Road. It is thought that the barn may have been the original farmhouse known as Chesiltons in the seventeenth century. The farm and barn were both listed, but nevertheless demolished in 1963/64 to be replaced by Rectory Way and Eleanor Grove.

Right: A 1930s advertisement for Pool's Dairy, proclaiming it to be the 'Oldest Dairy in the District – Established over 25 Years'.

Below: Cannons Cottages near the junction of Long Lane with Edinburgh Drive in 1984. At one time known as Pantile Cottages or Pretty Corner, their age is uncertain. They were part of Cannons Farm, which was demolished in the nineteenth century, and in recent years have been refurbished, while their gardens have given way to new houses.

Church Farm as painted by local artist W.G. 'Bob' Martin, whose work has been exhibited at the Royal Academy. Situated on the corner of Swakeleys Road and Long Lane and facing St Giles's Church, it was originally part of the Swakeleys estate. In 1937 it was acquired by Ralph Potts Guy along with Milton Farm, Tipper Farm and Ickenham Hall, and from 1940 to 1944 it was used as the local Home Guard headquarters. The farm buildings were demolished in 1946 and replaced by a parade of shops.

The entrance to Long Lane Farm, *c.* 1972. Built around 1700, it became part of the Swakeleys estate in 1869, and, when that was auctioned in 1922, the farm was purchased by Edward Dalton. The property remains with the family, is still a working farm, and operates under the name of Dalton's Dairies Ltd.

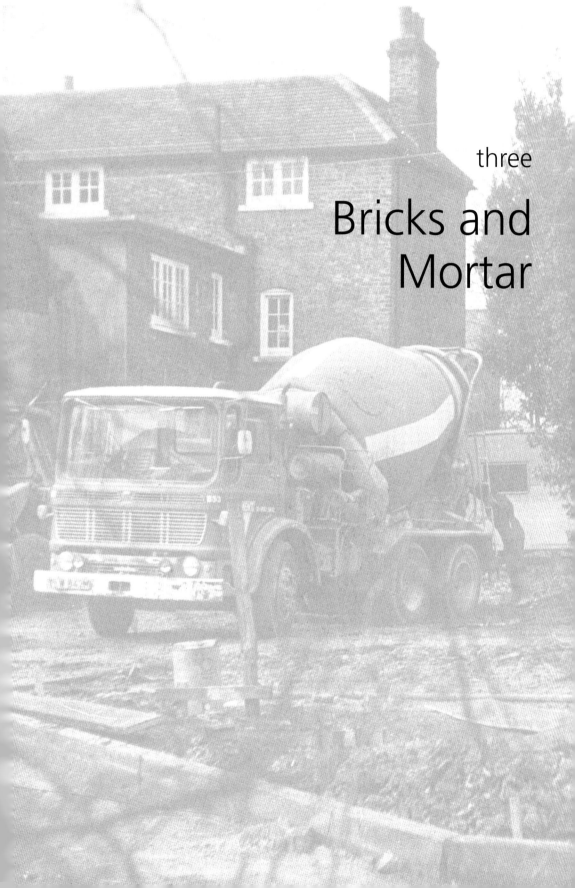

three

Bricks and
Mortar

The imposing west front of Swakeleys House, once described as one of the finest examples of a seventeenth-century Jacobean mansion in the country. The Grade I listed building replaced an earlier structure dating from the early 1300s. It was completed in 1638 by Edmund Wright, who became the Lord Mayor of London in 1640 and was knighted a year later. The next owner, Wright's son-in law Sir James Harrington, was a commissioner at the trial of King Charles I, and when the monarchy was restored in the person of Charles II, he fled to France in 1660. Soon afterwards Harrington's wife sold the property to Sir Robert Vyner who was made Lord Mayor in 1674, thus becoming the second London mayor to have resided at Swakeleys.

The north and east front of Swakeleys, described by diarist Samuel Pepys as 'a very pleasant place' after his visits in September and October 1665 – the year of the Great Plague. Apparently the purpose of Pepys's visits was to borrow money from Vyner (a leading goldsmith) on behalf of King Charles II, who had attended Sir Robert's mayoral banquet at the Guildhall. Unfortunately, Pepys was obliged to record a diary entry on 15 October – 'We went, he and I into his garden to discourse of money, but none is to be had'.

The house forms a magnificent backdrop to cricket on its front lawn during the late 1950s, when owned by the London Postal Region Sports Club. From 1927 it belonged to the Foreign Office Sports Association, who staged fixtures with local cricket clubs including Uxbridge and Ickenham. The grounds also provided a splendid setting for other sports, particularly croquet, and the All England Croquet Championships were held here in the 1890s when the tenant was Arthur Gilbey. The Gilbey family was renowned for its wine and spirit business, and Arthur also achieved prominence when he became High Sheriff of Middlesex in 1912.

By comparison with the summery scene above, Swakeleys appears to be a house for all seasons with its snow-capped gables and chimney stacks in December 1981. But the jewel in Ickenham's crown, for all its stately appearance, belied the fact that for many years the building had deteriorated into a lamentable state of decay – a condition that, happily, was rectified a few years later.

Swakeleys entrance hall and finely carved screen erected by Sir James Harrington, *c.* 1655. The triple-arched wooden and plaster screen was painted to give a marble and stone effect. A bust of King Charles I on top of the central arch is, in this picture, partly hidden by the chandelier, and the side arches are surmounted by two cherubs bearing shields of arms.

To the right of the screen is an elegant eighteenth-century marble fireplace – the largest in the house. Three busts adorn the mantelpiece – one of Ben Jonson in the middle, flanked by those of John Milton and James Harrington. The wrought iron fire back bears the date 1695.

Ickenham Lodge in the early 1900s. Situated on the corner of Swakeleys Drive and Long Lane, the lodge stood at the entrance to one of the main carriage drives to the house, and was the home of the head gardener.

Swakeleys Lodge, on the corner of Swakeleys Road and The Avenue, in 1970. Originally a pair of cottages that were converted into one residence, the lodge was positioned at the other principal entrance to Swakeleys House. In 1809, Thomas Truesdale Clarke senior purchased the property, which was used as a gamekeeper's cottage. Two massive piers supported the ornamental gates at the entrance, one of which survived and can just be seen behind the fence.

A rare picture of the frontage of Buntings, built in the late eighteenth century next to St Giles's church. For many years, the large house was the home of John and Charlotte Gell. She used a private footpath and gateway between Buntings and the church, and among the many bequests in her will was one of £200 to the rector for improvements to St Giles. A new Buntings was built in 1920 to replace the original house. It was set further back and incorporated some of the old cellars in the form of a sunken garden.

The Gell Almshouses, Swakeleys Road – an attractive row of five flint and brick cottages built for Charlotte Gell in 1857. Originally intended as retirement homes for her domestic staff, they eventually became available to the poor and needy senior citizens of Ickenham, provided that they met all the requirements of her will – one of which stipulated that they must be members of the Church of England.

Above: Orchard Cottage, Long Lane – a picturesque sixteenth-century building owned by Parish Councillor B. 'Floppy' Cowne. During the First World War, Mr Cowne allowed the house and grounds to be used for charity bazaars, and part of the orchard for a school garden to supplement wartime food shortages. During the 1930s, Cowne's Orchard, as it was often called, opened a tea-garden to cater for the many city dwellers who flocked to Ickenham by rail to spend the day in the countryside. The house was demolished in 1935, and Ickenham Library built on the site in 1962.

Right: Young Linda West amid the rubble that would eventually become the front garden of her parents' new house in St George's Drive in 1952. She is now the owner of the property. The road was one of many new developments taking place in Ickenham around this time.

The Cottages standing behind the pond. On the right is No. 4, which served as Ickenham's general shop from the mid–nineteenth century and as a post office from 1881.

Ickenham Hall, Glebe Avenue as it was in the late 1940s. Although cottages stood on the site around 1400, the present house was built around 1740 by the Shorediche family. Archive records list seventeen different occupants from then until 1947, including the Crosier and Hilliard families, Charles de Winton Kitcat, Dame Maude Lawrence and Ralph Potts Guy. Middlesex County Council purchased the house and 5½–acre site in 1948, converting it first into a community centre, then a youth centre and finally a youth theatre, when a new building was erected at the rear of the house in 1968. This theatre was the first of its kind in the country.

In 1974, it was decided to construct a single-storey connecting building between the house and theatre, and the project took two years to complete. This picture was taken in 1975, and shows Theatre Director John Sherratt clambering over the rubble as he keeps a watchful eye on the builders' progress.

This was the finished article. The attractive linking building became known as The Bistro, and the theatre had previously been christened The Compass by John Sherratt in 1974.

Ickenham village hall, designed by architect Clifton Davy, was built on farmland in 1926. The hall was opened on 8 January 1927 by Princess Victoria, sister of King George V. Owned and operated by the Village Hall Association under the leadership of George Richman, it has been used as a school, bank, polling station and a British restaurant in the Second World War, as well as a venue for dances, concerts and meetings of all the local organisations. This 2002 picture shows two Association committee members, Joan Parkin (left) and Dorothy Ansell, outside the hall which had just been re-roofed with new tiles.

A 1980s photograph of The Soldier's Return, High Road. Built in 1828 as a cottage and a blacksmith's forge, it has functioned as an inn from 1850. Since then several modifications have been made, including a change of picture on the pub sign.

The oldest of Ickenham's public houses, the Coach and Horses, pictured in 1989. Some parts of the building date from the sixteenth century. Many alterations have taken place over the years and the ancient barn, once a smithy, was demolished to make room for a car park. The Coach, as it is known locally, played an important role in village life during the nineteenth century when used as the venue for a Manor Court, where offenders were tried and sentenced by the Lord of the Manor.

The Fox and Geese, High Road in 1994. This building replaced the original hostelry that began life in the late 1800s, when two cottages were converted into a beer house. The blacksmith's shop, which was an extension to the inn, closed in 1924 and was used as a cattle shed before being converted to a lounge bar in 1925. And when Ickenham High Road was widened in 1934/35, the old public house was demolished.

The entrance to RAF West Ruislip in High Road, pictured in 1978. Built on the grazing meadows of Home Farm, it opened in 1917 as No. 4 Maintenance Unit, known locally as the Four Stores. The United States Air Force occupied the station from 1955 to 1975, when the US Navy took over. In the early 1980s, many of the buildings were demolished and a new housing estate, erroneously named Brackenbury Village, was established on part of the site.

A Second World War picture of members of the AFS (Auxiliary Fire Service) with their equipment on the sandbagged forecourt of Ivy House Cottages, near the corner of Milton Road. Several buildings in the village were adapted to play a part in the war effort. ARP posts were set up at various points including Swakeleys Road and the Glebe Estate, while a searchlight battery was installed in the grounds of Swakeleys House.

four

Tracks
in the Wilds

Railway gangers with one of the station staff at Ruislip and Ickenham Station in the late 1920s. The station served both the Great Central and Great Western Railways and opened on 2 April 1906. Situated on the Ickenham and Ruislip boundary, it was eventually renamed West Ruislip.

Another group working (or posing) on the tracks at Ruislip and Ickenham in the early 1930s. The gentleman second from the right is William Huse, whose wife Mary was a member of the well-known Winch family.

This striking photograph of a GWR goods train passing through West Ruislip en route for High Wycombe was taken in early 1948 by CRL (Lewis) Coles, who was a member of the Ickenham Society of Model Engineers.

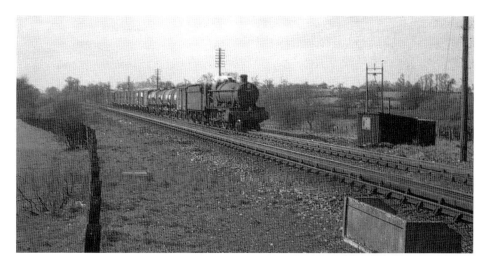

Twelve years on (between 1960 and '61) and the age of steam is coming to an end. Another goods train heading towards London approaches the station from the opposite direction, and may be one of the last steam trains to be captured on camera. In 1947/48, London Underground extended its Central Line to West Ruislip, resulting in the station undergoing a complete transformation. The Central Line tracks and platforms were constructed on the old approach road, the former station buildings and footbridge were demolished and a new entrance and booking hall catering for London Transport and British Rail passengers, opened on the High Road Bridge.

After the changes to the station, it was the turn of the rolling stock. This April 1960 picture shows the difference between the old and the new. The early 1930s Standard-type train on the right, being phased out, looks decidedly dated compared to the streamlined version standing alongside.

A Metropolitan Railway BTH electric train with 1st- and 3rd-class saloons stands on the up line at Ickenham Halt in 1906. The short wooden platforms could accommodate only three carriages at a time, so longer trains had to stop twice. Ickenham's first station was almost a non-starter. When the parish council asked the Uxbridge authority for a halt to be built, one councillor, probably unaccustomed to venturing into darkest Ickenham, was disparaging about the idea of a station 'out in the wilds'. But, fortunately for the residents, one was built and opened on 25 September 1905.

Almost fifty years later, this January 1953 scene from the up-line platform, shows very few changes. The platforms, extended in 1922, were now made of concrete, and the Metropolitan train has a more up-to-date appearance. To the left of the bridge is the small booking hut that opened in 1910, where passengers had to queue in the road for their tickets.

This June 1953 view from the bridge looking down the line towards Uxbridge is typical of a rural wayside halt, with trees and meadows bordering the station fences. The wooden huts acting as waiting rooms were still in use up to 1971. Both platforms are deserted except for the stationmaster and one or two passengers.

Above: Ickenham's original booking hut was fifty years old when this picture was taken in 1960. Nothing appears to have changed except that a modern red telephone box has replaced the old white kiosk installed in 1926. (Photograph by C. Horsey)

Left: The station in 1983, having experienced a complete makeover in 1971. In addition to the new frontage and indoor booking hall, commuters could now enjoy the added luxury of covered stairways to both platforms. A far cry from the days of the country halt! Another plus was the provision of a safety barrier outside the entrance, but the public telephone box was removed – which just goes to prove that you win some, you lose some.

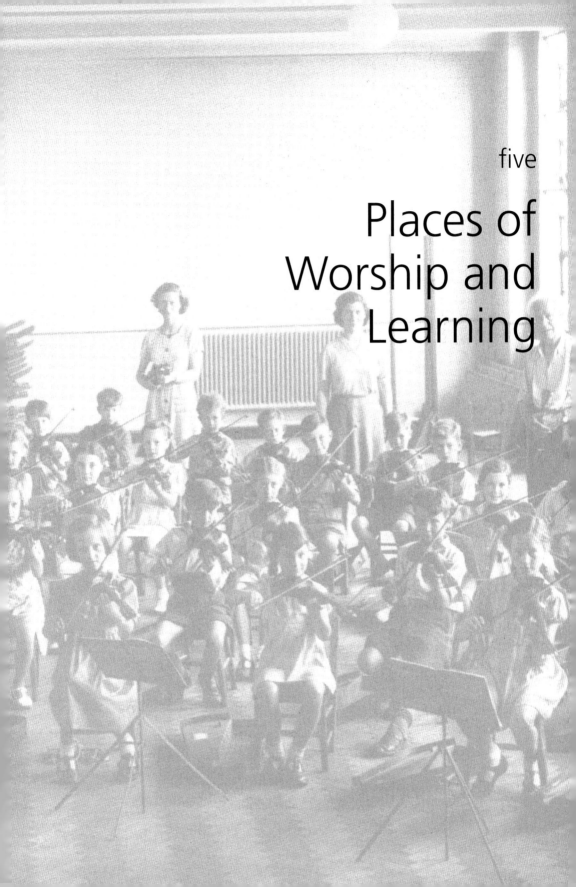

five

Places of Worship and Learning

A floodlit St Giles's church on Christmas Eve 2002. Ickenham's fourteenth-century parish church is a most attractive flint and brick building. Its small timbered belfry containing three stationary bells chimed by independent hammers supports a dwarf spire topped with a gilded cockerel. Many architectural additions and modifications have been made since 1500, when a wooden porch was added on the south side of the nave. A long, broad north aisle was added between 1575-80 and a mortuary chamber known as St John's Chapel in around 1645. Many treasures are housed within the church, including a veined marble sculpture of a shrouded baby who died in 1665, a seventeenth-century carved oak font, a 600-year-old stone coffin lid – the only one of its kind found in Middlesex – and various historic brasses, fine silver and registers dating from 1539, which record the first rector as John Payne.

The church and churchyard under a carpet of snow in January 2003. On the right of the picture is the Grade II listed Crosier family memorial. The railing surround and restoration of the tomb were completed with assistance from English Heritage.

The cast of the church nativity play in December 1983. From left to right: Janine Shotto, ? Douglas, Kirstie Austin, Hazel Crane, Heather Francis, Joanna Austin, Nicola Cameron, Astrid Capp, Jacqueline Parks, Sara Davies and Victoria Maltby.

Six members of St Giles's thirty-two-strong choir with choirmaster John Miley rehearsing for their performance at the Royal British Legion Festival of Remembrance at the Albert Hall on 13 November 1982. The service was attended by HM The Queen, the late Queen Mother, Prince Charles and the late Princess Diana. From left to right, back row: Daniel Ralph, John Miley, and Tim Mottershead. Front row: Colin Ayres, Neil Faulkner, Jason Reid, Bret Barnett. Neil and Jason were bishop's choristers, and Jason is now a priest. The choir sang at other Royal Remembrance Services at the Albert Hall, and also appeared on television.

St Giles's Flower Festival organiser Gill Roker poses on a tombstone with an eye-catching display prepared for the September 1989 festival. Patron Saint Giles was depicted in a forest setting, and flowers characterising twenty different saints decorated the church. Gill (a Chelsea Flower Show Gold Medallist) has been flower arranging at St Giles since the early 1980s, and continues to win medals at Chelsea.

St Giles's organist and choirmaster for the past twenty-four years, John Miley tries out the new Allen digital electronic organ in June 1993. Looking on is Paul Ayres, a finalist in the BBC's Young Composer of the Year competition in 1992. Paul, whose first music teacher was John Miley, had composed a seven-minute work for two organs titled *Memoriamley*, which had its world premiere at the church on 26 June 1993. Later, it was performed in St Albans Cathedral. After graduating from Oxford, Paul became a professional organist and composer, and was assistant organist at St George's, Hanover Square, London.

St Giles's church hall in a sorry state after being gutted by fire in April 1995.

Almost three years later, in January 1998, a new building has risen from the ashes of the old hall. It was restored and improved at a cost of £250,000, which included £100,000 raised by the church and community. While the restoration work was in progress, many of the hall's regular uses had to find alternative venues for their meetings. From left to right: Revd Philip Robinson, who became Priest in Charge of St Giles on 25 January 1995, Brian Reid, chairman of the Hall Management Committee; and Colin Kershaw, chairman of the Rebuilding Committee.

Above: The former Congregational church in High Road, known originally as the Independent Chapel. It cost £160 to build and opened on 3 November 1835. As a branch of the Providence Congregational church in Uxbridge, it was serviced from there until 1919. The founder was William Brickett, whose son David was enrolled as one of the first Sunday school pupils and eventually assumed leadership of the chapel.

On 9 May 1936, children were among those laying bricks at the stone-laying ceremony for the new Ickenham Congregational church in Swakeleys Road. The former building in High Road had finally proved inadequate to accommodate an increasing congregation. The rector of St Giles, Revd James B. King, is seen here reading the lesson. Mrs Perry, the granddaughter of original founder William Brickett, laid one of the foundation stones, as did Revd Bouch and David Pool (on behalf of the children of Ickenham).

This is the impressive building that ascended from the foundations shown above. It opened in late 1936 and was eventually renamed the United Reform church.

Opposite below: In early June 1935, a large gathering assembled at the chapel to commemorate the centenary of their Sunday school. Many former inhabitants of the village returned for this reunion of members who had attended the school in previous years. The church's celebrations continued throughout the year and in November guest speakers at the Village Hall included Uxbridge ministers Revd Luther Bouch, JP, and Revd F.L. Riches Lowe.

Ickenham's first purpose-built school was erected at the corner of High Road and Austin's Lane, on wasteland of Ickenham Manor. Known as the Church of England school, it opened in 1866. Prior to this, children were taught in the front room of Home Farm at a cost of tuppence per week – a charge that very few parents could afford. The school closed in 1929 in preparation for road widening and was demolished in 1934.

Pupils grouped in front of the school entrance in the early twentieth century. Back row, extreme right: headmaster Mr W.A. Lee (nicknamed Gaffer by the children). Fourth row, extreme left: teacher Miss Harrington.

Mr Lee sitting in the centre of another school group in the first part of the twentieth century.

This picture of similar vintage shows Miss Harrington on the extreme left and Mr Lee on the right by the fence.

Mr Lee again poses with his pupils and an unidentified schoolmistress on the extreme right. The boys in the front row are holding a slate inscribed 'Ickenham School No. 2'. It is thought that members of the Winch and Sims families are among the children as well as future Ickenham historian Morris Hughes.

The wording on the slate in this picture is 'Ickenham School, 1916'. It is uncertain if the gentleman in the boater and spectacles is an ageing Mr Lee, but Morris Hughes is definitely somewhere among the pupils.

Ickenham High School for Girls, pictured in 1957. Once described as 'Ickenham's answer to Cheltenham and Roedean', the school opened in December 1927 with thirty-five pupils and Dora Howard Rose as its Headmistress. Dora, who preferred to be known as Miss Howard, originally began classes in the former Congregational Chapel in 1925, then moved them to High Trees, a house in Oak Avenue, and finally purchased the Old Rectory, an eighteenth-century house in Swakeleys Road. Although sometimes described as Georgian, parts of the building dated from the Queen Anne period and earlier.

One of the classrooms in the converted four-storey house. The lowest floor was a semi-basement, while the fourth floor was in the roof and used as a dormitory for boarders. In 1939, the school was expanded to accommodate more girls and a preparatory school for boys was introduced. At the start of the Second World War, the basements were reinforced for use as air-raid shelters – a fact that Miss Howard always emphasised in her local press advertisements. The school closed in 1964 (with Dora still at the helm) and was then demolished to make way for new roads and housing.

The organisers of the High School Old Girls' Association reunion at the United Reform church in July 1983. Over seventy ex-pupils attended, including some of the first (in 1925) and the last (in 1964). From left to right are: Joan Peck, Boo Musgrave, Gillian Kirby, Pauline Bennett, Rosemary Fennell, Phylis Varley, Joy Smith, Barbara Jackson and Mary Purdom (maiden names).

More smiling faces at a later reunion in May 1997, organised by Barbara Smith, a pupil from 1945 to 1953. The lunch held at the village hall was attended by eighty 'old girls' and two 'old boys'. From left to right: Barbara Smith, Joan Davidson, Joan Kirby, Diana Spencer and Pat Cragg (proudly wearing her school badge).

The official opening of a new council school in Long Lane on 22 February 1930 by Lady Hanworth – standing next to Chairman of Governors Maj. E.W.C. Flavell. The rector of St Giles, Revd D.W.W. Carmichael (fifth from right) shared the platform with the first headmaster, Mr A.H. Streets, and other officials. The school, known as Swakeleys, first opened its doors in late 1929 when older children were moved from the former village school. In 1952, the boys were transferred to Abbotsfield School in Hillingdon, leaving Swakeleys as a secondary modern girls' school. But they also moved to Abbotsfield in 1973, when the building became an adult education centre.

Swakeleys' fourth annual sports day on 27 May 1936. Major Flavell is seen presenting the House Trophy (the Flavell Cup) to the Harrington House captains. Vyner House, who had won the cup in 1934 and 1935, was the runner-up.

The Breakspear Junior School, Bushey Road. It opened on 19 May 1937 with 200 pupils, after lessons had been held in the village hall during construction. The first headmaster was James Ward, who held office for twenty-five years, followed by Peter Ettling, who served even longer. The present incumbent (only the third headmaster since 1937) is Philip Rutter.

Excellent costumes and scenery feature in this Breakspear School production of 1946. Carole Watt stands on the extreme left.

Thirty-four budding violinists making music in the school hall in 1947. Looking on are headmaster James Ward (back row, extreme left) and violin tutor Hullar Brown (back row, extreme right), with other members of staff.

A scene from the school nativity play of 1947.

Pupils posing in costume at the opening of Glebe Primary School, Sussex Road, in April 1952. Starting with a relatively modest intake, the school roll had topped the 200 mark by 1974.

Their Royal Highnesses the Earl and Countess of Wessex at the ceremony commemorating the school's Golden Jubilee on 22 April 2002. Prince Edward (who had visited Ickenham to reopen the refurbished Compass Theatre on 12 November 1990) unveiled a plaque on the Glebe School wall to mark the occasion. The royal couple then made a tour of the building and met pupils of every class.

Right: Vyners School, Warren Road, which opened on 12 January 1960 with 247 pupils and 13 teachers. The first headmaster was Trevor Jaggar. As the building's completion date had been delayed, the first pupils were accommodated at St Mary's Grammar School, Northwood Hills from 9 September 1959.

Below: Some of the 130 newcomers in the first intake of September 1960 signing the Great Book of Vyners – a practice that became a school tradition.

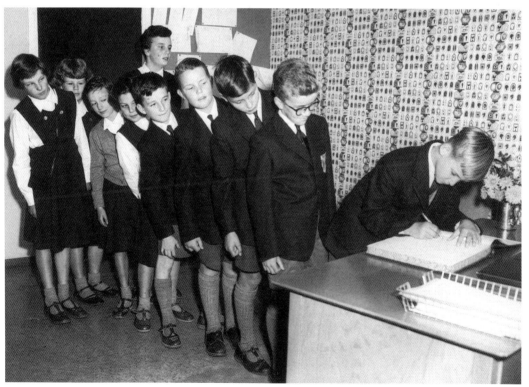

Above: The Staff and Boys *v.* Fathers cricket match at Vyners in 1961. The umpire (back row, extreme left) is music teacher and former West Drayton cricketer Norman Lane. Headmaster Trevor Jaggar (back row, centre) was himself a cricketer of some repute.

Left: Television presenter Judith Chalmers opening Vyners' second annual fête on 23 June 1962. The man in the white suit sitting in the front row is Uxbridge MP Charles Curran. Trevor Jaggar is already padded up, waiting to be bowled at in the nets by pupils, fathers, guests and also Miss Chalmers — all in a good cause!

Vyners' third annual speech day, November 1962. Former England rugby captain and a school friend of Trevor Jaggar, John Kendall-Carpenter is presenting a prize to Anthony Heritage, who went on to Cambridge University. Deputy headmaster Richard Fox is second from the left, next to headmaster Trevor Jaggar.

Norman Lane, Head of Music at Vyners, conducting the school senior choir at a rehearsal for a Haydn and Mozart concert in March 1965. Norman, who died in 1986, was a giant in local music circles. He conducted the Sine Nomine Singers, Hillingdon Sinfonia Orchestra, Uxbridge Musical and Dramatic Society and Ickenham Strings, which he founded while at Vyners. He was also an examiner for the Associated Board of the Royal Schools of Music.

Vyners School rugby team, 1968/69 season. From left to right, back row: B. Gornall, G. Barrett, B. Barrow, M. Broomhead, A. Knibbs, M. Plesch, S. Coombs, P. Docherty, C. Worsley, and R.A. Parr. Front row: K. Dumbleton, S. Senior, T. Foot, K. Stewart, M. Smith (captain), C. Quirk, R. Pimm, M. Kilpin, N. Tucker.

Vyners School Swing Band with its founder and conductor Perry Parsons (middle row, extreme right) in 1989. All the members of the original band, formed by Perry in January 1988, are present. Since then, many different charities have benefited from the band's concerts at the school and other venues. The band also performs regularly at the Festival of Ickenham Gala Day in the grounds of Swakeleys House.

Vyners pupils with headmaster Brian Houghton (back row, extreme left), preparing to bury a time capsule beneath a new classroom under construction. This piece of history was compiled by Head of History and Politics Peter Creber in May 1996 and included examples of music, currency, fashions, food and stamps. The capsule also contained a review of life at Vyners and records of interviews with residents of Hillingdon and Ickenham.

Douay Martyrs School, Edinburgh Drive. This Roman Catholic senior school opened in 1962 with 450 pupils. Twenty years later, the roll totalled 862. The school celebrated its silver jubilee in May 1987 and the guest of honour was the late Cardinal Basil Hume. Douay's first headmaster Mr P.E. Burke and Mayor Donald Mitchell were also in attendance.

Colin Dexter, the author of *Inspector Morse*, signing books for Douay Martyrs pupils on
6 December 1991. Mr Dexter, whom headmistress Marie Stubbs described as 'an awfully modest,
very bright man', had previously given the students tips on solving crosswords (he had been the
National Crossword Champion on three occasions), but pupils were unable to trick him into
revealing Morse's first name – which remained a secret.

Prizewinners at a special Douay Martyrs ceremony in January 2000 attended by Uxbridge MP John
Randall, when prizes were awarded for both academic and community work. The school has greatly
expanded over the years since 1962 and now serves all of Hillingdon Borough. After a new building
had been erected on the Edinburgh Drive side of Long Lane, the school extended across the road
and acquired part of the former Swakeleys School, naming it the Cardinal Hume Campus.

six

Trading Places

Ickenham post office in the 1920s. Standing in the doorway is Miss Ellen Butler, who became postmistress when her father Daniel died in 1903. He had managed the combined post office and general shop from 1890 and she continued in the same vein until 1939.

John R. (Jack) Inwards (centre) with two of his staff outside his newly acquired garage and petrol station in Swakeleys Road in 1925. The assistants are displaying the latest models of BSA motorcycles. Jack was born in Harefield and moved to Ickenham when his father bought a smallholding, Bythorne House in Glebe Avenue, that was once part of the Swakeleys estate.

The garage in around 1930 with other shops that had been built on the parade, including Stedman and Clarke's estate agents office; the Bon-Bon, a confectioner's and newsagency owned by A.G. Rayner; and F.E. Smith's butchers shop.

Opposite below: The blacksmith's forge attached to the Fox and Geese hostelry in High Road. This 1910 picture shows Welshman Llewellyn Wood busy practising his trade, while still finding time to pose for the camera. Llewellyn, who took over the blacksmith's shop from William Montague in around 1902, proudly advertised 'Horses shod on the most approved principles'. Later he transferred his smithy to the great barn at the rear of the Coach and Horses.

The magnificent seven – an impressive display of Inwards' range of Citroën cars in the early 1930s. Jack (centre) has just established a Citroën dealership, while his sister Rose (third from left) helped with the business. The enterprising Jack opened a second branch with showrooms at Ruislip, dealing in Standard Triumphs and Vauxhalls which were advertised on local cinema screens. The Ickenham garage eventually reverted to a petrol station and motor body shop. Jack's sons joined the business, which then extended to branches in Hillingdon, Marlow and Greenford. The company was sold in 1980, six years after Jack's death, and now the Tichenham Inn occupies the Swakeleys Road site.

Great Central Parade, High Road in 1930. It derived its name from the nearby Great Central Railway and was built in 1926 opposite the approach road to Ruislip and Ickenham station. It consisted of nine shops, including those of Ickenham's first fishmonger H.G. Knight (No. 1), G.S. Wright Radio and Cycle Dealer (No. 4) and Shaw's Boot and Shoe Store (No. 8). Knight's shop was taken over later by A. Pearce.

Frank Shew's greengrocery in Swakeleys Road, soon after opening in 1928. A family concern, the shop was managed by Frank and his wife Lucy, who were helped by brother Alfred and his wife Marie, seen here with an assistant. During the Second World War, Shew's reputation grew as customers came from far and wide when news got around that the shop had a supply of bananas – which in wartime were tantamount to gold dust. The crowds were so big that, in order to be fair to his regular customers, Frank organised two separate queues – one for locals and one for outsiders.

A happy group inside the shop in around 1953 – probably smiling at the thought of being the first shop in the area to have installed a refrigerator. Left to right: Frank's mother Rose, Alfred, Nora Osborne, who assisted in the shop for twenty-five years, and Frank's son, Dudley Shew.

This 1963 shot of a shiny new lorry is evidence of entrepreneur Frank's venture into the haulage business, in addition to greengrocery. He started in the 1920s, selling door to door with the aid of a horse (called Daisy) and cart. Then he traded from a pitch in the grounds of Pool's Dairy at Ivy House Farm, before opening his first shop. In 1946, he purchased a second shop in Swakeleys Road and for a time his sister managed a third in Ruislip Manor.

The new shop in the early 1970s, indicating that Frank's son Geoff was part of the firm. Geoff entered the business at the age of fifteen, assumed control when his father retired in 1977, and disposed of it in 1988.

Geoff Shew appearing to be master of all he surveys, as he prepares for the opening of the refurbished shop in 1985.

The shop after reopening, showing the changes effected by the revamping.

Another Ickenham entrepreneur was Alec Hamer, seen here in 1949 outside the shack in Glebe Avenue which became his second shop. The first was a shed in his back garden. Alec traded in this building, known as The Hut, from 1940 until 1957.

Alec at work in the gas-lit hut, *c.* 1950. By now, he was stocking other products and the shop became a general store for the residents of the Glebe estate. He worked a twelve hour day with a two-hour lunch break, and also served as an air-raid warden at Burnham Avenue ARP post during the war years. Between 1951and '52 the hut was burgled with monotonous regularity – intruders breaking in through the sides, the door, windows and roof, forcing Alec to carry his stock home every night.

Youngsters queuing outside Alec's newly built shop in Glebe Avenue on Saturday 19 October 1957. They are eagerly awaiting the 2.00 p.m. opening – performed officially by Alec's grandson, four-year-old Jim.

Meanwhile, the staff behind the counter await the rush which resulted from a promise of free sweets for everyone. From left to right: Alec, his son Bob, Alec's wife Lilias, Bob's wife Betty, their son Jim, and assistant Mrs Harris.

Alec outside his new premises in 1960. By now he had extended the business to include toys, cycles and various other goods.

In May 1989, Bob proudly displays photographs of the shop's history before setting them up in a front window to commemorate the firm's fifty years of trading. Bob had been involved in the business since childhood and took control after his father died in 1973. Then, with help from his sister Dorothy, he carried on until reaching the golden anniversary, and sold the business soon afterwards.

Mr Noel Edwards loyally waving the Union Jack as he decorates Saich and Edwards' shop, High Road in preparation for HM the Queen's Silver Jubilee in June 1977. Algernon Saich, a brother of Cyril who owned Home Farm, opened the shop originally as a grocery, confectionery and tobacco business under the name Ickenham Green Stores in the 1920s. But eventually the general shop changed direction, dealing in antiques and collectables.

Seven years on, in June 1984, and another new dimension has been added in the form of fireplaces, second-hand timber and scrap metals. Saich and Edwards' yard now encompasses the former Congregational Chapel (left) which had been used as both a cafe and furniture store since closing in the 1930s.

Brian Saich outside his men's outfitters shop in Uxbridge prior to its closure in June 1978. His father Leonard – another brother of Algernon and Cyril – had opened the business in 1930 in addition to a similar one in Swakeleys Road. Brian took over in 1950.

Alan William (Bill) Imber and his son Bob (on the left) outside their estate agents office in Swakeleys Road in January 1999. Bill, who served in the Royal Artillery during the Second World War and fought in the North Africa and Italy campaigns, came to Ickenham in 1956. He launched his estate agency as a one-man operation on Parkfield Parade, High Road in 1962, moved the business to Swakeleys Road in 1970, and expanded it in 1983. Bob joined the firm in 1977. The agency was sold in 1999 and Bill died in June 2002, shortly after the death of his son, who, after retiring, had moved to Somerset.

seven

Dad's Army Lives On

A wartime picture of Ickenham's Home Guard at their Church Farm HQ in Swakeleys Road. Known as 'A' Company, 14th Middlesex Battalion, their Commanding Officer was Maj. W. 'Sandy' Sanderson (front row, sixth from the right). The Home Guard was formed in May 1940 under the name of Local Defence Volunteers (LDV), with men aged seventeen to sixty-five. A quarter of a million volunteers nationwide joined during the first week and, at its peak, the force numbered two million.

Ickenham's 'A' Company was part of a big Wings For Victory parade on 6 March 1943. The procession is seen here in Wellington Road, Uxbridge after marching through the town. Despite the image depicted in television's *Dad's Army*, this was no raggle-taggle outfit. Gone were the days of drilling with broom handles and walking sticks and sharing one rifle between a whole company. These men took their responsibilities seriously, knowing that they were Britain's last line of defence and, should the unthinkable have happened, they certainly would have made their presence felt.

A captivated audience at a children's Christmas party given by Swakeleys Home Guard Association at Breakspear School in 1946. The Association was formed in September 1944 for members and ex-members of the Ickenham Home Guard to 'perpetuate the esprit de corps which was the outstanding feature of the Home Guard during its activities'.

The Association's first annual dinner in 1948. When the threat of a German invasion had receded, the nation's Home Guard was disbanded on 11 November 1944, and the men of 'Dad's Army' hung up their guns for the last time. Major Sanderson, John Monk and Jesse Castley are among those standing; Douglas Watt is seated on the left of the front table with Harry Fairbairn on his left.

Members of the Association leaving St Giles's church after attending their annual Church Parade in 1952. In the porch doorway are Douglas and Terry Watt, whose son-in-law Alan Noad is the Association's chairman. From left to right, front row: Jesse and Vee Castley, Charles Bridge, Stan Dickenson.

Having restricted its first annual dinners to men only, the Association then decided to invite the ladies and hold dinner dances. From left to right: Brig. E.W.C. Flavell, Mrs Flavell, John Monk (past chairman), Mrs Peggy Monk. Brig. Flavell, a previous president of the Association, formally opened its present headquarters at a purpose-built clubhouse on 21 May 1954. The one hundred or so members meet here regularly on social occasions, and are also actively involved in raising money for local charities.

eight

Leisure
Activities

The Land of the Windmills was one of the artistic items presented by the pupils of Miss Norah Eyre's dancing school at the village hall in June 1935. Among the girls in the front row are Margaret Harrington, Hazel Robinson and Jean Mackay.

Members of the Ickenham and District Society of Model Engineers at their first exhibition on 14 May 1949. A track had been laid for their locomotives in a field off Swakeleys Road. The society was formed in September 1948 by C.F. Clarabut and H.C. Piggott and held its first meetings at the old ARP huts, then Ickenham Hall and the Memorial Hall before settling in its present headquarters behind the Coach and Horses public house. Among the many enthusiasts are Messrs. Wilson, Whitfield, Sexton, Tarrant, Piggott, Caton, Clarabut, Sales, Dunn, Fairbairn, Scott, Milligan and Ward.

One of the society's first members, Peter Fairbairn, with his five-inch gauge 4-4-0 locomotive *Maid of Eastcote* at the society's 1950 exhibition held in the village hall and an adjacent meadow. Payment for the use of the field was fifty Player's cigarettes!

The official opening of the clubhouse at the society's new home near the Coach and Horses on 18 June 1955. On the dais, the then chairman Peter Fairbairn is introducing Councillor Lt-Com Staples (extreme right) who performed the ceremony, opening the door with a 'golden' key.

An added attraction at the society's 1955 Open Day was this 1931 Sentinel steam wagon *Goliath* standing by the Village Pump. For the photographer's benefit, two society members are posed 'turning' the wheels. The one in overalls is Alan Martin, who was involved with traction engine restoration.

Open Day in around 1965. Laurie Green (right) demonstrates his newly built boiler and partially completed chassis to interested onlookers. Since then, many major improvements have been made on the site which, by 1998, had received 100,000 visitors. A continuous ground-level track was opened in 1969, a station named Ickenham St Giles in 1982 and a signal box in 1993. Public interest in the miniature railway is now so great that 1,000 rides are sold on every Open Day.

Girls from a local dancing school demonstrate their art at an Open Evening in Ickenham Hall Youth House in the early 1960s. The house was used by young people for many varied activities, including drama, dancing, music and photography.

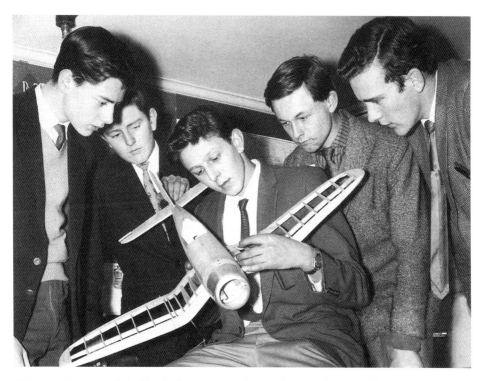

Other regular users of the Youth Centre were a Young Farmers Group, a Film Society and an Aero-Modelling Club, whose members are pictured here examining an example of their work.

Minister for the Arts, the Rt. Hon. Jennie Lee (centre), widow of Aneurin Bevan, meets Susan Beavan (left) and her mother K.M. 'Kit' Beavan (right) at the Youth House in 1966. Kit was appointed Warden of the centre in 1959 and Susan was the producer of the Young Argosy Players who rehearsed there. Jennie Lee returned on 26 October 1968 to open the new Youth Theatre built behind the house, and again (as Baroness Lee) on 16 October 1976 to open the linking buildings.

The 'Compass Theatre on Tour' performing at Harefield Hospital in 1984. For many years the company, under its new name Compass, had taken the theatre to the people, touring far and wide, including regular trips to Emden and Schleswig in Germany. Their Artistic Director was John Sherratt, appointed in 1968, who gave twenty-four years of dedicated service before leaving in 1992. Hundreds of young people benefited from his tutelage, many going on to make their careers in the professional theatre.

Four leading players from the cast of *The Secret Diary of Adrian Mole*, one of John Sherratt's last productions at the Compass in May 1991. From left to right: Daniel Soanes, Sarah Jones, Anne Jones, Jason Richards.

John Sherratt's last appearance with the 'Compass Theatre on Tour' at the Middlesex showground, Uxbridge, in 1992. Seated at the Yamaha organ is internationally acclaimed organist Ena Baga, who, like her famous sister Florence de Jong, appeared regularly at the Compass from 1972 onwards, accompanying around fifty classic silent films that were screened there.

Chris Owen (left) was appointed to run the new Youth Education Unit at the Compass in 1992, when the theatre group received a new name: Magnetic North. From left to right: Chris, Cleo Felstead, Gregory King-Underwood and Donna Shilling in January 1993.

One of Magnetic North's early productions was *Shakers* in March 1994. The cast consisted of the four girls seen in the picture. From left to right: Lisa Foley, Rachel Pass, Laura Young and Janie Manzoori.

Five flappers from the Pastiche company's production of *The Boy Friend* at the Compass in January 1997. From left to right: Ickenham girl Elaine Verweymeren, Rebecca Llewellyn, Kay Mulligan, Vanda Simmons and Roma Ridley, daughter of the group's producer Jean Hobson. Jean and her husband Alan were residents of Ickenham for many years.

Members of the Studio Theatre company at a break in rehearsals for *Talking Heads* at the Compass in October 1998. The group comprised players from John Sherratt's original company who stayed together after his departure, renaming themselves Studio Theatre. From left to right: Sarah Westlake, Clive Room, Elly Beevor and Wendy Robinson.

Members of 1st Ickenham Scout Group in 1968, displaying the Stilwell Shield which they won competing against eighteen other troops within the Borough. The shield was awarded for skills in all aspects of Scoutcraft, and has been won by the 1st Ickenham Scouts on very many occasions.

The 1st Ickenham at a group ramble along the Grand Union Canal from Uxbridge to Harefield in 1982, with Assistant Scout Leaders Howard Heyd (centre) and Peter Tilsed (front row). Howard's father Rayner Heyd served as the group's Scout Leader for fourteen years in three separate spells.

Right: The 1st Ickenham won the Stilwell Shield again in 1992. From left to right, back row: Patrol Leader Richard Jennings, Daniel Dunstan, Assistant Patrol Leader Mark Connelly. Front row: David King and Sebastian Bleasdale. The troop was formed in 1929, when meetings were held at St Giles's church hall. Their first permanent hut was burnt down two months after being erected in 1935, and a replacement built in 1936 suffered the same fate twenty years later. During the Second World War, it was requisitioned by the War Office to house soldiers manning the searchlight battery in the grounds of Swakeleys House.

Below: Ickenham scouts and cubs in 1997, preparing for St George's Day on 23 April, when, traditionally, the Scout Movement nationwide engages in parades and church services. They are pictured at their present headquarters in Community Close, which was officially opened on 9 May 1959. From left to right: Johnathan Byrne and Thomas Fawssett (2nd Ickenham Cubs), John Warrall (1st Ickenham Scouts), Matthew Dodd (1st Ickenham Cubs), Richard Lomath (1st Ickenham Scouts), Lewis Kendall and Mark Douglas (2nd Ickenham Beavers).

A happy group of girls of the 2nd Ickenham (St Giles) Guides Company, attending their church parade at St Giles in September 1960. The company was formed in February 1945.

More smiling faces as Angela Scripps, Sheila Lambert and Susan Thomas of the 2nd Ickenham Guides help to entertain old people at a 1962 Christmas party in the church hall. For their traditional Christmas Good Turn, the Guides prepared tea and organised games and community singing. The party was financed with money raised at the Company's coffee mornings.

The 2nd Ickenham Guides in holiday mode at their Summer Camp at Blacklands Farm, East Grinstead, in August 1965. This was their first camp as a whole company and their captain, Miss P. Varley, was taking her captain's licence. She relinquished the captaincy in December 1967.

The 2nd Ickenham Brownies looking pleased at having raised £41 at their 1983 Christmas sale, for the *Uxbridge Gazette* Body Scanner Appeal. *Gazette* Deputy Editor Paul Harrington poses with the girls after receiving the cheque at St Giles's church hall in January 1984. The scanner was required for cancer treatment at Mount Vernon Hospital, Northwood.

Members of Ickenham's Women's Institute, whose branch was formed in 1924, celebrating at their Golden Jubilee Fayre in 1974.0

One of the WI's many activities was drama and they participated regularly in local drama festivals. The picture shows the cast of a 1980 One Act Festival production *Covenant with Death*, which was also presented at the village hall. The splendid costumes were designed by Pat Byrne, the group's producer.

Ickenham Village Townswomen's Guild enjoying a garden party held at the home of Kitty Smith in August 1993. Kitty (sitting in foreground) hosts the event annually. The Guild was formed in May 1984 by Elsie Fry, Pamela Barnard, Margaret Catchpole and Cynthia Mallinson. There are eighty-six members in the group, whose activities include gardening, handicrafts, music, bridge, social studies, walking and charity work.

The Townwomen's Guild's eleventh birthday party, held at the village hall in May 1995. The then chairman Betty Ackland is seen cutting the cake, in accordance with their usual custom.

Ickenham Cricket Club in July 1978. From left to right, back row: Dick David, Dick Stevens, John Roberts, Ken Stewart, Peter Hewitson, Dave Boothman. Front row: Peter Cook, Andy Scott, Jim Room, Richard Hayward, Alan Roberts. The team had won the Uxbridge Twenty-Over Knockout Cup for the second year running, and went on to complete a hat-trick of wins in 1979. They had also won the Truman's Seventy-Five League championship in consecutive years – 1976, 1977 and 1978. After joining the Thames Valley League, all three Ickenham elevens won their respective divisions in 1980.

The team celebrate their win in the final of the cup in 1978. Man of the match Richard Hayward pours champagne into the cup, held by top scorer Jim Room.

Another picture of the team in their heyday. From left to right, back row: Geoff Wilkins, Dave Boothman, Andy Scott, Jim Room, Steve Lynch, Seead Hatteea. Front row: Dick David, Alan Roberts, Malcolm Sully, Richard Hayward, Phil Evans. In its early years, the club played on the Rectory Field and in the Milton Farm area, before moving to its permanent home at Oak Avenue in 1928. After renting the ground from the former Middlesex County Council, the club was able to purchase it for £5,000 in the late 1950s.

The Ickenham team of 1993. Standing on the extreme left is ex-Middlesex player Robin Sims. Robin, whose grandfather and father both played for Ickenham, signed for the County side in 1989, but returned to his home club in 1995. He had joined Ickenham as a fifteen-year-old in 1986. During his first season with Middlesex, he was called on as a substitute fielder in the England *v.* Australia Test Match at Lords, and caught Aussie Captain Alan Border – a feat of which he is constantly reminded!

Ickenham St Giles Football Club in the late 1950s. Their coach/manager Frank Caulkett is on the extreme right and his son Tony is in the front row, extreme left. The club was formed in the early 1950s from boys of St Giles's church, where Frank was a chorister. Later in the decade, the team joined the Uxbridge League, playing first at Rockingham Recreation Ground and then on Ickenham Green.

The team celebrate a Cup win in the 1956/57 season. Tony Caulkett is in the centre of the front row.

Above: Another happy occasion for the team in the 1957/58 season, when they finished runners-up in the league's second division. Frank Caulkett is on the extreme left with son Tony sitting next to him. In 1966, the club merged with another local team, Ickenham North End, and became Ickenham Sports.

Right: On 13 June 1995, Frank Caulkett receives the Middlesex County Football Association's Meritorious Service Award at Yeading Football Club. He was one of only ten people to be honoured with this award since 1883. Although his dedication to junior football had already spanned forty-five years, Frank continued to work as the club secretary until he and his wife Irene were obliged to move into a Northwood residential home. He died in 2003, aged ninety-two.

Children participating in a Literary Fancy Dress Party at Ickenham Library on 18 June 1980. The event was organised by the local branch of the National Women's Register, which claims to be 'for the lively minded woman'. Formed in the late 1970s, the branch's activities include discussion and book groups, and visits to theatres and places of interest. From left to right, back row: Mark Adams, Simon O'Brien, Sarah Hockey, Nicky Zubac, Douglas Brodie. Middle row: Joelle Newson, Anthony Pearson, Deborah Powell, Victoria Johnson, Katy Johnson, Joshua May, -?-, Lucy Powell. Seated: Tom Elliott, Paul Williams, Jane Williams, Olivia May, Michelle Hockey, Joanna Brodie.

Members of Swakeleys Bowls Club with their guests from the Windsor Royal Household Bowls Club and Chiltern and Thames Club on 7 May 1985. The Swakeleys club hosted a three-way tournament to coincide with Prince Philip's visit to Swakeleys House, seen in the background.

Wayfarers Tennis Club coach Tim Blackman holding a training session for young hopefuls and their parents at the Swakeleys Drive club in May 1994. They are using a new court built at a cost of £35,000, raised from club monies and fund-raising events. Wayfarers now has six courts and an expanding membership.

Members of the Fox and Geese rugby team and their supporters enjoying a final drink before leaving to play two matches in Wrexham, North Wales in April 1986. No doubt they had a reason for wearing colourful Caribbean shirts at a Welsh rugby game, but it is not immediately apparent!

Ickenham and Swakeleys Horticultural Society's Spring Show on 3 April 1993 at the village hall. From left to right: Show Judge Fred Harvey, Society Chairman Brian Robinson, Roger Trigg, winner of the Best Bloom trophy for which he received the Bill Naylor cup from the mayor, Councillor Alf Langley. The society, which presented over 250 exhibits at the show, was formed in 1945 under the name Ickenham Allotments Society, and has organised annual events ever since.

nine

People and Events

Above: Ickenham's well-known Winch family, *c.* 1910. From left to right, back row: William, Charles, Arthur, James junior. Front row: Polly, father James and Mary.

Left: Young James Winch at work in the grounds of Swakeleys Manor, where he was an apprentice gardener, around 1911.

Another well-known name in Ickenham is that of the Sims family. Joseph Sims is giving his granddaughter May a ride in his firm's cart at the end of the nineteenth century. The name 'J. Sims & Sons, Builders' is painted on the side. Young May grew up to have a granddaughter of her own, Betty, who is married to former newsagent Bob Hamer.

The Brewin family in the grounds of Swakeleys, *c.* 1938. From left to right, back row: Harold, Frederick and William. Front row: father Edward, Mary, Gladys (William's wife) and mother Louisa. Edward and Louisa were steward and housekeeper at Swakeleys from 1927 until 1939. Mary's daughter Susan is married to the *Ickenham Church News* editor, David Crane.

Volunteer Poppy Day collectors at the Village Pump in November 1932. A fenced-off area in the foreground represents a miniature Field of Remembrance.

Dame Beatrix Lyall, President of the Mothers Union, opening a bazaar in aid of St Giles's church hall on 26 October 1935. With her are the rector Revd J.B. King, Mr A.G. Burr and David Pool (people's warden). The hall was built in October 1934 at a cost of £2,000, and £60 profit realised at the bazaar completely cleared the debt, which had been greatly reduced by the villagers' generosity.

Ickenham Brownies gather round the mountain ash tree planted by Mrs David Pool on 16 November 1935 to commemorate King George V and Queen Mary's Silver Jubilee. The event was organised by the Brown Owl, Miss Sawyer, and the dedication of the tree made by Sir Wolstan Dixie of Ickenham Manor.

A rare treat in wartime was this belated Christmas party at the village hall on 7 February 1942, organised by the wardens of Ickenham's ARP Post 12. Over 150 children attended the party, which was subsidised by residents and local tradesmen.

Yorkshire-born Flying Officer Jim Foley volunteered for the RAF in March 1941. After training as a navigator in Canada, America and then England, he joined 460 Squadron, No. 1 Group, Bomber Command, flying Lancasters. In May 1943 he was posted to 156 Squadron – part of Pathfinder Force of voluntary air crews – and completed twenty-seven operations over Germany. Transferring to 608 Squadron No. 8 Group, he took part in fifty-five raids in Mosquitos in the dual role of navigator and bomb aimer. Jim was awarded the Distinguished Flying Cross in December 1944 for 'navigational skills and calmness under fire from heavily defended targets, especially over Berlin, and for displaying the utmost fortitude, courage and devotion to duty'. During a brief spell as an instructor with 69 Squadron at RAF Northolt, he met Ickenham girl Peggy Sheffield, whom he married in April 1945, and then set up home in the village. After demobilisation, Jim took up accountancy, became a Company Secretary and, eventually, a Director of a Public Company. A keen cricketer, he played for Ickenham from 1946 to 1966.

Londoner Harry Berry enlisted in the 5th Field Regiment, Royal Artillery in September 1939. Following service in India and Malaya, he was captured in Singapore in 1942 and held in Changi jail before being transferred to Omori POW Camp, Tokyo. After 3½ years, he was liberated by US Marines on 29 August 1945. Back in Civvy Street, Harry resumed his pre-war job as a feature writer on the *Star* newspaper. Then, in 1953, he became Public Relations Manager for BEA (now British Airways) where his work entailed dealing with celebrities from Sir Winston Churchill to The Beatles. With his wife Gwen, whom he had married in 1940, and daughter Linda, Harry moved to St George's Drive Ickenham in 1952, choosing No. 29 for his house number. Having been freed from the POW camp on 29 August, he believed it to be his lucky number! Harry nursed his wife through Parkinson's disease until her death in 2003, and he died in January 2004.

Above: Children from Ickenham and Hillingdon Primary Schools at a Victory Party in June 1946 to celebrate the end of the Second World War (in August 1945). They are grouped in front of Swakeleys House, where an army lorry is evidence of the searchlight battery stationed there during the war.

Right: The rector of St Giles, Revd F.G. Evans, admiring the memorial window dedicated to the Ickenham 'A' Company, 14th Middlesex Regiment of the Home Guard. The dedication was made during the Swakeleys Home Guard Association's annual memorial service in June 1951, when the window was unveiled by former Commanding Officer Maj. W. Sanderson, MM. Also present at the ceremony was the Association's president Brig. E.W.C. Flavell, DSO.

The unveiling ceremony of the Gospel Oak commemorative stone in Swakeleys Road on 29 January 1950. When the surrounding estate was being laid out, the builder W.S. Try had marked the site of the tree for preservation. The ancient oak which denoted the Ickenham parish boundary was a feature of ceremonials in Roman times. The memorial tablet made of Derbyshire wood and Hopton stone bears the inscription 'Here in medieval days beneath this Holy oak or Gospel tree came once a year the curate and people to invoke Divine Blessing upon their forthcoming crops'. The stone was unveiled by Mr Willoughby Gardner of the Middlesex Archaeological Society. From left to right: W.S. Try, council chairman G.A. Suter, JP, Willoughby Gardner, and John Poole, Clerk to Uxbridge Council.

Three members of the Home Guard Association manning their darts stall at the Breakspear School Fête in June 1953. The fête was part of Ickenham's celebrations during Coronation week. From left to right: Charles Bridge, Stan Dickenson, secretary Jesse Castley.

The highlight of the Coronation celebrations was a procession of twenty-two decorated floats led by a mounted herald and the band of the Air Training Corps. Starting from the Community Centre in Glebe Avenue, the procession was launched by stage and screen star Bobby Howes. An added attraction was the appearance of Sir Wolstan Dixie, Bart of Ickenham Manor who sat in the stocks outside the Coach and Horses while spectators pelted him with eggs and tomatoes – all in a good cause!

This vehicle carried a tableau depicting Henry VIII and his six wives – portrayed by members of the Women's Institute.

Uxbridge MP, the late Michael Shersby (a former pupil of Breakspear school) with Ickenham Festival organiser David Millen (right) at the Village Pump during the 1977 celebrations for HM the Queen's Silver Jubilee. They appear to be discussing the absence of the pump handle, which had been removed for safe keeping by the local authority in 1921 and has not been seen since! Fortunately, a replacement similar to the original was fitted in March 2004.

HRH the Duke of Edinburgh accepts a commemorative book at Swakeleys House on 7 May 1985, after reopening the refurbished mansion. On the right is Keith Chamberlain, who, with fellow residents Paul Newson and Simon Kreiger, was responsible for restoring the house to its former glory. Since the 1950s, it had fallen into disrepair and in 1980 Keith and his two colleagues formed a consortium in an attempt to rescue the building from massive redevelopment proposals. Five years and several million pounds later, their Herculean efforts came to fruition when the restoration was completed in March 1985. The Duke congratulated the three partners personally and Keith received a letter of thanks from Buckingham Palace. Then, in 1988, came the icing on the cake when his company Swakeleys House Ltd won the Country House Award for the best conversion of a listed country house.

Pupils of Breakspear and Glebe Schools wave to the cameraman as they anxiously await Prince Philip's arrival. He had visited Swakeleys House in November 1977, describing it then as being 'in a terrible state'.

Their waiting is rewarded when the Duke goes to meet them. Amid a sea of Union Jacks, one little girl wants to greet him with open arms, while a young lad gets a prize photograph for his snapshot album.

Left: Television presenter Sue Cook receiving flowers from young Hazel Crane at the St Giles's Autumn Fair on 20 October 1984. Sue, whose childhood home was in Burnham Avenue, was a pupil at both Glebe and Vyners Schools before going to university. She returns to Ickenham frequently to support local causes.

Below: The late Betty and Keith Briggs, who died in 2003 and 2004 respectively. A former mayor of Hillingdon and Ickenham Ward councillor, Keith took a great interest in local affairs, being president of the Horticultural Society and a member of many other organisations including the St Giles' Watch Committee. After war service as a sergeant in the Royal Engineers, he married Betty in 1945. Before moving to Ickenham, he was a semi-professional guitarist with Southend's premier dance band, working with guest artists, pianist George Shearing and bass player David Nixon. Betty also served as an army sergeant in the Second World War and afterwards spent much of her life in service to the local community.

Right: Dennis Edwards (right) and Walter Beauchamp at Ickenham Residents' Association's fiftieth anniversary show at the village hall in June 1985. The Association, whose aims are 'to preserve and enhance Ickenham', was founded in 1924. It lapsed for a few years, but was re-established in 1935. Dennis, a former chairman of the association, is an expert on local and railway history, and the author of many books on both subjects. He now lives in Wales.

Below: Hilda and Morris Hughes on the occasion of their Diamond Wedding in 1989. Morris was born on 10 January 1905 at No. 4 Old Cottages – Ickenham's first post office – and attended the church school in High Road. He and Hilda (born 18 December 1901) began their married life in Uxbridge, but moved back to Ickenham in 1931. Morris wrote and painted, subsequently becoming an authoritative local historian. He was the author of many newspaper and magazine articles and a book on Ickenham history. Later, he admitted hating history at school! Morris died on 4 September 1989 and Hilda on 28 June 1999, leaving two sons and six grandchildren.

Left: Ilford-born Freddy Staff has lived in Ickenham since 1958 and spent fifty-six years in the music profession. In that time he has played trumpet with the dance bands of Harry Roy, Geraldo, Joe Loss, Billy Ternant, Eric Winstone and the Skyrockets. He then became lead trumpeter of the Syd Lawrence Orchestra for sixteen years, and now directs his own orchestra, the Manhattan Swing Band. During an illustrious career, he has toured and performed with international stars Judy Garland, Barbara Streisand, Shirley Bassey, Tony Bennett, Tom Jones, Sammy Davis Junior, Jack Jones and Englebert Humperdinck.

Below: Another trumpeter, the late, great Roy Castle, who teamed up with the Vyners Swing Band for a sell-out charity concert at the school on 21 September 1991. They are seen here rehearsing for the show which raised £1,500 for Chiltern and Hillingdon Cheshire Homes. The band's conductor, Perry Parsons, is standing left of Roy, who played several solos, sang and tap-danced to an audience of over 450 people. The concert was the Vyners Band's fiftieth public performance.

Against the background of Swakeleys House, the British Airways band plays at the Festival of Ickenham in June 1996. The festival was inaugurated in October 1975 by David Millen, who, with his committee, has organised the biennial event since 1976. Numerous local societies and tradespeople participate in a week of diverse activities, culminating on Gala Day when the whole community comes together to enjoy the festivities. These include a procession around the village, 'all the fun of the fair' in Swakeleys grounds, a concert by the Vyners and Perry Parsons Bands and a spectacular fireworks display as a grand finale.

Members of Ickenham's National Women's Register celebrate after their float won first prize at the festival in June 2000. From left to right, front row: Sue Banks, Maureen Jockell, Phil Wood. Back row: Diana May and Karen Humphreys.

In December 1999, for the first time in its history, Ickenham village hall is fitted with a clock to mark the millennium. The original asbestos roof tiles were replaced in 2002. Many improvements have been made to the hall since the 1940s and it remains in constant use, having around 750 letting periods per year. In 1998 hire charges were £8 per hour, somewhat higher than in the 1930s and 1940s, when the charge was 45s for a Saturday night dance and 35s for a concert or play. On weekdays, it was even cheaper!

The Gospel Oak rises again! Having stood for centuries, the ancient tree was gradually reduced to a stump that finally toppled over. But, on 3 December 2003, a new oak of the genus *Quercus robur* was planted behind the memorial stone. Chairman of the Residents' Association Peter Daymond is adding the final spade of soil, watched by an interested group of Ickenham people, including David Crane (extreme left). David has edited the *Church News* since 1999, after taking over from John Hillier.

Right: Ickenham resident Tim Noad with one of the three panels he designed for the Chapel Royal ceiling at St James's Palace to commemorate HM the Queen's Golden Jubilee in 2002. Tim, who is the son of Janet and Alan Noad, is Herald Painter at the College of Arms. His work has been exhibited in St Paul's Cathedral and various London galleries, and he has published books on illumination and calligraphy. He also designed the sovereign coin issued only for Jubilee year, and the Jubilee Medal which was awarded to around 360,000 people, including Princes William and Harry.

Below: Another of Tim's commissions resulted in this magnificent painting of Swakeleys House, to mark the mansion's 350th anniversary in 1988.

Other local titles published by Tempus

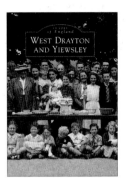

West Drayton and Yiewsley
JAMES SKINNER

This fascinating compilation of over 200 old photographs illustrates the history of these two Middlesex towns, charting their progress from agricultural communities of golden cornfields, to the coming of the railway and the industry it would bring.
0 7524 2841 1

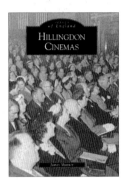

Hillingdon Cinemas
JAMES SKINNER

An invaluable collection of archive photographs providing a glimpse into the history of cinema in this London borough during the mid-twentieth century. This book is sure to appeal to all who remember the important role moviegoing has played in the history of Hillingdon.
0 7524 2610 9

Middlesex CCC 100 Greats
ROBERT BROOKE

Middlesex CCC has produced many fine players from professional stalwarts such as 'Old Tom' Hearne to amateurs like I.D. and V.E. Walker. This book concentrates on the players who made the present club synonymous with attractive and successful cricket.
0 7524 2746 6

London's Railways
K.A. SCHOLEY

In the past, the railway fed and heated, while today, it helps to access the suburbs adding to the power and influence of the capital. Illustrated with images dating from 1850 to 1950, London's Railways demonstrates to us the central place of rail travel in London and the importance of this to local people.
0 7524 1605 7

If you are interested in purchasing other books published by Tempus, or in case you have difficulty finding any Tempus books in your local bookshop, you can also place orders directly through our website

www.tempus-publishing.com